My Grief Journey
Stories and Illustrations

Steve Nauman

ISBN: 1514638525
ISBN-13: 978-1514638521

To everyone serving as a caregiver
for your loved one

CONTENTS

ACKNOWLEDGMENTS

Thank you to all the wonderful health-care providers throughout Laura's times of sickness.

Extra special thanks to Dr. John Kincaid and Dr. Alan Bierlein: you both did so much to help us; to the outpatient infusion nurses: your knowledge, care, and concern will remain in my memories; to the Goshen Home Care and Hospice team: you all demonstrated what compassionate care really is.

And thank you so much to all of our faithful encouragers—what a blessing you have been.

INTRODUCTION

My wife, Laura, and I had only been married for about nine months when she injured her shoulder. At first we tried therapy and rest—and more therapy and rest—but her injury would not heal and continued to grow worse and more painful. Over the next few years, she had several surgeries on the shoulder and eventually had the shoulder joint removed and the bones fused together. During that time, she also began experiencing more problems with weakness involving her arms and legs.

After a few more years of continued progressive weakness, her doctors diagnosed her with a motor neuron disease. The most widely known motor neuron disease is probably ALS, commonly called Lou Gehrig's disease. Hers was like a slower form of that disease and displayed many of the same symptoms.

During those early years, God taught us both so much about learning to be content in whatever our circumstances were. By 1988, Laura was using a power wheelchair to get around, and that's when she received a service dog, the first certified service dog in our county. Laura called her "Roxi." That dog could pick up dropped items, pull open the refrigerator door, bring in the mail, and do so much more.

This was also about the time that Laura started having Bible clubs for children in our neighborhood. She was so good at teaching those children in a way that they enjoyed. Eventually, she no longer had the strength to invest in the children; plus, we had to move from that small house to a larger one that would better accommodate her physical needs.

She was able to continue having a ministry with Roxi, as she was still able to go to the mall, and Roxi would "mouth—hand" to interested people a beautiful brochure that we had printed: *Roxi the Wonder Dog*. The brochure shared some of what the dog did for Laura and also told about our lives and our faith in Christ.

Laura's physical condition continued to decline: to the point where, by 1995, she was confined to bed and had difficulty breathing. To everyone involved in her care, it appeared that death was very close.

Then on September 2, 1995, with no one around, at six thirty in the morning, God chose to completely heal her body. She was immediately able to breathe deeply on her own; she had full use of her arms and legs; and she was walking without any assistance! Her doctor came to see this "miracle" with his own eyes, and he said, "You either have to call it a miracle or just shrug your shoulders."

As incredible, rare, and wonderful as her healing was, we were stunned and somewhat overwhelmed, because just about every aspect of our lives also changed with the healing. For example, for several years I had been known to some as "the guy married to the woman in the wheelchair, who has Roxi!" Also, Laura's driver's license had expired years before, when she could no longer drive, so she had to prepare for both the written and road test to receive a new driver's license. Another challenge for her was that roads, buildings, etc. had changed so much in those years that she didn't know where most places were anymore.

The news of her healing quickly spread throughout our local area and beyond, with TV news crews filming interviews. There were also several articles in the local newspapers. On a national level, the *700 Club* TV program sent a reporter and crew to film a news story about Laura's miracle from God, and they did a wonderful job—with all the credit and glory going to God alone.

We were also bombarded with invitations to many churches, clubs, and various groups to share our testimony about the miracle. For the first several months we turned down all of those invitations, because we both had so much to adjust to and to learn about each other and our relationship. So we took a little time to spend together, catching up on some of the wonderful and fun things of life as we pondered how to properly use our situation to glorify God. We once again printed a brochure, but instead of a picture of Laura in a wheelchair with her service dog, it said, *Miracles Happen*, and it had a picture of Laura on a motorcycle!

Next, we were able to develop a program outline and started accepting those invitations from all the different churches and groups. We would show the very nicely done video story that the *700 Club* gave us; Laura would share some of her personal testimony; and we would play several songs, with Laura on the guitar and me playing the banjo and singing.

As long as we had permission to tell the story exactly as it happened, making sure all the glory and credit went to God, we would accept the invitations to share what He had done in our lives. We shared our testimonies nearly two hundred times over a six-year period: to groups as small as twenty people and to several that had over eight hundred in attendance.

The details of that miracle are way too extensive to incorporate into these stories about my grief journey, but it was necessary to give you a glimpse to help you (and me) understand the incredible relationship we shared as husband and wife.

After the healing, Laura had seven years of vibrant health and accomplished more in that short time than some accomplish in a long lifetime. She learned how to play guitar, rode dirt bikes, built a barn, made wood crafts, did leather carving, and enjoyed card making and oil paintings. She got several horses, trained them, and rode them. She started hunting and fishing, and in 1999, we recorded a music CD titled *Simple Praise from the Land of Goshen*. But her greatest joy of those years was the after-school Bible clubs she taught in some nearby schools. She called them J. O. Y. Clubs, which stands for: Jesus first, others second, and yourself last.

In early 2003, she started "wheezing" sometimes and started having trouble focusing her eyes. Her doctor said that she had asthma and started treating her for that. On April 13, 2003, she collapsed and was rushed to the hospital by ambulance. Our local hospital stabilized her, and within a few hours, she was sitting up, feeling alert, and talking with me. But the doctors there were concerned with exactly what was wrong with her, so they transferred her to a large hospital in Indianapolis.

When I arrived there to see her, she was in the neuroscience ICU—and on a ventilator! I remember standing there, almost in shock, looking at her and wondering what had happened. As I stood there, the neurology team of doctors came toward me, and I said, "All this for asthma?"

They explained that she didn't have asthma; she had an autoimmune disease in which her body was attacking itself. The doctors told me that it was treatable with medications and with some other specialized treatments. She experienced multiple complications as her health gradually declined over the next eleven years. On March 1, 2014, Laura, the love of my life, took her last breath, and my grief journey began.

1 ADVICE FROM A FRIEND

Second Corinthians 1:4 teaches us that we should comfort each other with the same comfort that God has given to us. When I started my grief journey, I didn't see how I could ever comfort someone else in his or her grief, because I was searching for comfort myself. To me, my grief could be described as severe emotional trauma, and in an imaginary way, it put me in an "emotional ICU" (intensive care unit).

In reality, an ICU focuses on all the critical aspects of the patient's health, sometimes even providing life support. Then, when the patient is stable, he or she is usually moved to a "step-down" unit, where some form of rehabilitation begins. In the "emotional ICU," where I found myself during the first week or two of grief, my emotions were not capable of receiving comfort (which I think represented the rehab aspect of my recovery). But my rehabilitation process was about to begin.

About three weeks after my wife's passing, I received some very good advice from a friend. This friend had some real experience with grief. He had lost his daughter in a car accident, and then several years later, he had lost his wife of many years, to disease. He called me, and I remember well what he said:

"Did you receive some sort of grief resource book from hospice that gave suggestions on learning how to process and cope with the grief?"

I said that I had, and that I had read through it.

He then asked, "Did it suggest some form of journaling your thoughts and feelings?"

I replied, "Yes, I saw that, but I thought, 'That's for women,' and I turned the page."

He then encouraged me to consider a daily journaling activity to process the grief. I remember telling him that I had no idea what I would—or even could—write about if I were to try it. He told me that whatever I wrote was for my eyes only, so it didn't matter what I wrote about.

I then said that if any other person had suggested this to me, I absolutely would not have even tried, but since I had a lot of respect for our friendship, I'd give it a try.

That night I sat down with a pen and a pad of paper, wondering if I would be able to write about anything that I was experiencing. Well, my rehabilitation from grief started that night: I filled six pages! Many times as the weeks and months went on, I would have to stop and let the paper dry, because the water dripping from my eyes made the pages too wet to write on.

He was also right about those journals being for my eyes only, because the emotions and thoughts were so "raw," and at times confusing, that they wouldn't have made much sense to anyone else. But I was so thankful for the comfort that I received as a result of my friend's advice. For me, the journaling that I did every day for the first year of grief proved to be the single most helpful and healing activity of my grief journey.

Everyone's different, but for me, the daily journaling lasted one year. The day I started year two of my grief journey, I no longer felt the need to journal. I tried, but the page remained blank. That daily activity, which had proven to be a huge part of my emotional healing, was completed. At that point I started going back over my year of journaling, and that's where I found the thoughts, feelings, and ideas for these short stories pertaining to my grief journey. So just as the advice from a friend opened a door toward my healing and provided comfort in my grief, I hope that these stories will provide some insight, healing, or comfort for you as well.

JOURNAL

_____

_____

_____

_____

_____

_____

_____

_____

_____

_____

_____

_____

_____

_____

_____

_____

_____

_____

_____

_____

_____

_____

_____

_____

_____

_____

_____

_____

_____

2 THE GRIEF MAZE

Day after day...in a place you've never been, don't like, but are not allowed to leave.

I don't know if many others have feelings similar to those on their grief journey or if my experience was much different from everyone else's. But that's where I found myself a few days after my wife, Laura, passed away.

I'll first have to let you know something so that when I describe where I seemed to find myself, it will have more meaning:

I don't like cities.

I mean I *really* don't like cities. And the bigger they are, the more I dislike them. I'm not talking about the people in the cities; it's the big, tall skyscrapers that I don't like. I really don't know why either. Maybe if I were a builder or had some background in architecture, I could enjoy and appreciate those skyscrapers.

If I look at tall, majestic trees, I get a calm, peaceful feeling inside. If I look at tall buildings, I'm not impressed, and I get a very uneasy feeling inside. It's not severe like a panic or anxiety attack, but it's more like, "I don't get it; I've seen enough; let me out of here"—that type of feeling. In other words, it's not a place where I would ever choose to be.

After my wife's funeral, after everyone and everything I used to know returned to their respective normal, I found myself in what I refer to as a "grief maze." I would describe it as a usually dark, lonely, and very intimidating place. There was no way to turn back and not enter the maze, because there was a high, smooth wall separating me from life as I had known it with my wife. The maze was dark, because the walls in it were as high as the wall to my past. It was also very lonely, because there was no other person there but me. Also, it was a very intimidating place for me to be, because the walls were like skyscrapers—only there were no doors, windows, or even streets. There were no directions about where to go or if there was even a certain direction or a pathway out.

I instinctively knew that in order to survive, I had to start moving through the maze to see if there was a way out of it. I felt as though no one but God was allowed to go with me, so I continually asked Him to guide me, teach me, give me courage, and show me the way. It was very slow going at first, because as I started down one of the alleys, I would come to a dead end. Then I'd have to backtrack and try another alley, only to eventually encounter more dead ends.

Something else that made the journey so slow was that it was usually very dark in the alleys, because the skyscraper walls were so high and the alleys so narrow that the only time it was bright was when the sun was directly overhead. As soon as I started feeling like I was possibly making a little progress, other complications entered my maze. I called them the "waves of grief." When the first one hit me, it picked me up and carried me back to the start of the maze. I felt devastated. Just when I thought I was making some progress, I found myself right back at the start again, wondering if there really was a way out. I knew I didn't want to remain in that dark, lonely place, so I started out again.

As I journeyed, I was somewhat surprised to find that I recognized some of the wrong turns I had made on my first attempt. So I made it back to where I had been when the grief wave had picked me up—only this time it seemed to go much more quickly than it had taken me the first time. As I proceeded to make my way through the maze and to learn more about it, the grief waves continued to force me to start over again and again. Eventually, I remembered enough about the maze that I was able to almost run through it, more easily making it back to where I had left off.

As the months went on, I started to notice how much more light I had in the alley, because the walls had become much lower: to the point where I thought that if I had a short ladder, I would be able to see over the top of them! I started thinking that even if there were no end to this maze, at least it was no longer dark and intimidating.

After about a year of working hard to find the end of the maze, I looked around and wondered, "What happened to my maze? It's gone! I'm out, and I don't even know when I got out!"

So, does that mean that I've completed my grief journey? No, no, no. I think those illustrations only represented the most raw, severe, confusing, and completely unknown portion of my journey. I still have my moments of grief, but they're usually only moments, not the life-controlling periods of time like they once were.

This description of the grief maze is more than just an analogy. It accurately describes how I felt in the early days of grief. As I shared this with others, only those with personal experience with grief would truly and fully understand. The ways in which grief can change you— the way you live, think, and function (or don't)—is an absolutely incredible experience. Not being an emotional person, I never would have thought that the emotion of grief could control so much of my life.

Looking back at those times of severe grief also reminds me of how God loved and cared enough for me. Like Abraham's servant in Genesis 24, I can say, "'The Lord led me' on this journey."

And yes, He's still leading!

JOURNAL

3 SURPRISES OF GRIEF

I have to admit that before my wife passed away, I knew very little of what the level of grief from losing the one I was closest to—the one who was part of me—would be like. Even though this can be vastly different for everyone, I'll try to describe a little of what that loss was like—and the surprises of grief that followed.

For nearly twelve years Laura and I fought an enemy that had attacked her body. That enemy was called myasthenia gravis, an autoimmune disease that caused her body to constantly produce billions of antibodies that attacked and tried to destroy the ACH receptors at the nerve/muscle junction. In other words, it prevented the nerve signal from getting through to the muscle. Its regular area of attack would be the eyes, mouth, swallowing ability, and respiratory system. To complicate matters even more, her type was atypical, meaning that many of the standard methods of treatment did little or nothing to help.

As her primary caregiver, I started reading, studying, and learning everything and every detail that I could find about her medical condition. One of her doctors throughout the disease was a university professor, and his constant support, advice, and availability were a tremendous help. As the years went on and her health declined—with the final level being in-home hospice care—my job as caregiver grew to 24/7: always on call, always there or very close, and always available. I received a lot of personal satisfaction over the years in witnessing how the ability and strength that God gave me proved to be so helpful and necessary in her care. Even in the last stage, hospice, I felt like I was very necessary during those six months when the focus shifted to her comfort.

Here's where the surprises began.

Like many others, I don't have many memories of the funeral service or from that whole week. But a few days after the funeral, when everyone had left and the calls, e-mails, and visits had stopped, I was faced with something surprising. I call it the most "profound silence" I have ever heard, and when silence is profound, you *can* hear it!

After all the years of learning everything I could about caring for her, after all the calls and conversations with doctors, nurses, and other medical providers, and after the twenty-four-hour-a-day care that I gave her, life as I had known it was over. I felt as though I only had half a body left—my other half was gone and not coming back. Plus, after all those years of learning about and caring for my wife, I felt like I'd been fired! My services were no longer needed. Yet the care schedule was programmed into my brain, and my thoughts were still very much involved with her care.

So that was one of my first surprises: I was grieving the fact of no longer having her to care for. That didn't make much sense to my tired and confused brain.

During that first "alone" week, I received an e-mail from a friend who had lost his wife several years ago, and he said, "You're probably feeling pretty weak after losing your reason for being so strong."

I wrote back: "It's a little simpler than that. I'm feeling pretty weak after losing my reason for being."

In addition to the "profound silence," I was also surprised by the "profound aloneness." Picture it this way: I'm five years old, and it's my first day of kindergarten. I ride this giant yellow bus to the biggest brick building I've ever seen, and then I go inside to a big room filled with more strangers than I've ever seen before. Then, after a confusing day of wondering what I'm doing there, I somehow miss the bus ride home. There I stand, all alone. I don't know my address; I don't know my phone number; I don't even know my parents' first names. So I am completely alone, not knowing where I am, and wondering, "What do I do?" That's what "profound aloneness" felt like to me.

The next surprise of grief was a sense of "profound loss." It was obvious and simple to understand that I had lost my spouse—just as millions and millions before me have lost theirs.

Though my wife and I were never able to have children, throughout all the years we had together, we always felt like a large, complete family. After my wife was gone, the loss was so intense that I felt like she represented not only my wife but also my children and grandchildren. I had lost my entire, complete, large family! Of course, I was painfully aware of reality and knew for sure that I had "only" lost my wife, but those were the feelings I had to deal with.

These were the things that made me realize just how complicated and complex grief could be. Looking back on all that I experienced, I now realize that at the time of my wife's passing, I was physically and emotionally exhausted. But knowing now what I've learned about grief, even if I had entered this with a rested and strong body and mind, I'm sure that grief still would have had many surprises in store for me.

JOURNAL

_____

_____

_____

_____

_____

_____

_____

_____

_____

_____

_____

_____

_____

_____

_____

_____

_____

_____

_____

_____

_____

_____

_____

_____

_____

_____

4 THINGS GREW STRANGELY DIM

During the final six months of Laura's disease, she enrolled in home hospice care. We had access to the hospice nurses anytime, day or night, but I was her primary caregiver during that stage as well. At night I would nap in a recliner next to her bed so that I could quickly respond to any problems or struggles she might have.

One week before her passing, her condition started to deteriorate, and the complications started mounting. It was late on a Friday night when hospice sent in the highest level of oxygen concentrator they had, because her blood oxygen level was dropping too low. She was no longer able to swallow at all, so I had to suction her throat several times an hour during the day and almost constantly from about 10:00 p.m. to 6:00 a.m. (That was also when I named the suction machine "Hammering Hank." It was hard to believe that a machine the size of a lunchbox could make so much noise!)

By Monday morning, Laura, my wife of almost thirty-six years, the one I knew better than anyone in the world, was changing. By changing, I'm not really referring to her physical condition. Her "innermost being" was changing. She was still alert and aware of everything and everyone, but no *thing* was important, and every *one* was.

As I was giving her some medication through her G-tube, the words from an old hymn came to mind, because they described what I was witnessing: "And the things of earth will grow strangely dim in the light of His glory and grace." For the first time in my life, one word from that song jumped out at me, and that was the word *strangely*. The best way to describe it is to say that there was no thing, possession, image, or even taste that mattered anymore.

The next night was her last night at home, as she was scheduled to be taken to the hospital the following morning for "respite care," which was designed to allow me to get some rest. We talked that night with a sense that this was our last night together in our home. She thanked me for loving her, caring for her, and making her feel so special.

I told her that loving her was so easy, and caring for her felt like my calling from God.

Then Laura said something that showed me how very aware she was of the immediate future. She said,

"My suffering's almost over, and yours is about to begin."

I sort of dismissed it and just told her how much I loved her. Then she added, "God will help you through the grief, and all the answers to the questions and problems you'll have are in His Word. Let God teach you how to cry, because you will need to cry, a lot, and I know you don't cry."

At the moment she said that, I still didn't recognize the depth of what she was saying. Laura had a very complex mind; in fact, that's the part of her I miss the most. But it really didn't hit me until she had been gone a week or two. At that point I thought, "How did she know so much about the level of grief I would be experiencing?"

I thought of her words often as the almost never-ending tears were flowing from my eyes like water from a leaky pipe. (If God was teaching me how to cry on this grief journey, I certainly was a fast learner.)

As I try to figure out things now, I realize that even though she was the one I loved more than anyone in the world, I never let my emotions "get in the way" of caring for her. I guess that might be similar to the way a doctor, nurse, firefighter, or law enforcement officer has to maintain control of his or her emotions, regardless of how tense the situation is. I don't know if that was good, bad, right, or wrong; that's just the way it was.

Several months into my grief journey, I was talking with a man who was a Christian singer/songwriter. I told him about the morning when I had seen the things of earth grow strangely dim for Laura. He told me of a family friend who had over many years of her life collected certain ceramic figurines—to the point where she probably had a complete collection. She was very pleased with that collection and could tell you the story behind each of the figurines. When she was in her final days, he witnessed the same thing as the things of earth grew strangely dim for her.

He said, "You probably could have broken that woman's figurines, and it wouldn't have bothered her at all."

She, like Laura, was getting closer to the glory of God, and that's why the things of earth were growing dim. He shared with me that he later wrote a song about that experience and mentioned how, eventually, "things" are just taking up space.

I've heard of some people who, in their final days, say things like, "I wish I could have seen this or that or gone here or there, etc.," but Laura didn't display any of those thoughts. Even I, finding myself alone and being thrust into a new life that seemed to be controlled by grief, didn't have those regret-related thoughts.

But one thing I think of much more now than I did before is to not get overly concerned with collecting "things." Because someday all of those things will just be taking up space as the things of earth grow strangely dim for me—just as they will for you.

"For where your treasure is, there your heart will be also" (Matthew 6:21, NIV).

JOURNAL

5 FORMER SELF – NEW SELF

I never would have imagined that grief could have been so complex or even as life-changing as it had proven to be for me. As far as relatives I can remember, I've lost my great-grandparents, my grandparents, aunts, uncles, cousins, and some very special friends. When my father passed away, I thought, "Surely, this is grief." As far as my life experience had brought me at that point, yes, it was grief. But I experienced an entirely new and unbelievable level of grief when I lost my wife. The level of grief I felt takes nothing from the grief of losing other family members or friends. In fact, my father was the most incredible man I ever knew, and I loved and respected him deeply, making my grief over his loss great.

However, I am attempting to emphasize that I now more fully understand that, most likely, my mother must have experienced complex, maybe even life-changing grief, because she lost the one she'd been closest to for fifty-seven years. For me, in the grief of losing my wife, it was like I was in a place between my "old self" (whom I knew pretty well) and my "new self" (whom I was just getting to know). I don't even like to admit that, because it sounds like something you'd hear on one of those "everyone hold hands, have a good cry, and then laugh" talk shows!

Let me tell you how I realized where I'm at. When Laura passed away, I found myself telling people, "I wish I had my old brain back," because nothing in my thought processes was working the way it used to. My brain felt like a computer that had hundreds of windows or apps open all at once, accessing a different one every few seconds in rapid-fire order. To put it in terms I'm more used to using: my thoughts felt like a BB in a boxcar.

On top of that, I now had emotions that I had no experience in dealing with. I was not progressing very fast on my grief journey, because I was kind of stuck with trying to figure out how to get my "old brain" back.

About eight or nine months into my grief journey, I watched a movie on television about a young man who was starting his first year of college. He suddenly had a severe stroke that put him in the ICU for three weeks and into a rehab hospital for several months. Even though he was trying about as hard as a young, healthy person could, he still had many physical and mental impairments. It was very easy to understand his growing level of frustration with what seemed to be extremely slow progress. He met with a counselor to try to sort out his frustrations, and he eventually shouted, "I just want my old self back!" The counselor understood that he really was saying that he wanted his former life back. But that life was now gone, and no amount of hard work or searching would bring it back.

It was then that I realized that by saying, "I wish I had my old brain back," I was more likely meaning, "I wish I had my old life with Laura back." That "former life" was the life I had shared with Laura. I'm different now. I have new thought processes. I feel emotions that I never felt before. And the obvious part: I am now alone.

I'm sure I look about the same to people who know me, but much of me *is* different. Writing things like this is an example of the difference: I never would have or could have done this before, nor would I have been willing to have expressed and exposed my feelings.

The foundation of my personality, my core beliefs, and my moral fiber are the same, but I have to accept the fact that a lot of me is—and will be—different from my former self.

What exactly are all of those differences? I don't know. But they will gradually "come to be"—in time and with God's help.

JOURNAL

6 THE MOUNTAIN OF LOVE

Laura and I had a deep and complex love, and though I never thought about it while we were still "one," I now realize that few people have the awesome privilege of experiencing that special "oneness" that we had.

Looking back, it was the years of my wife's sickness (which included incredible ups *and* downs) that led us closer to God and so very close to each other. If we had been able to have chosen the plans and events for our lives, we never would have chosen the ones that God chose for us. At the beginning of our marriage, we never could have seen, heard, or even imagined the incredible life-changing events that would draw us so close to God and so close to each other.

Now I'm alone. I'm no longer on top of that majestic mountain of love that we so carefully climbed together. But we did climb that mountain *together*, with God guiding every little step of the way. We helped each other and held on to each other when one of us would slip, and God was always there, helping both of us. We made it all the way to the "summit" together, something that not many have accomplished.

Now God is with me as I make my way down the treacherous mountainside. As I carefully make my way down, I'm remembering so much about our thirty-six-year climb. Those memories cause me to say, "Thank you, Lord, for giving us the desires of our hearts, especially since we didn't even know what the desires that caused us to love so deeply would even look like. Amen."

> Love is patient, love is kind. It does not envy, it does not boast, it is not proud. It does not dishonor others, it is not self-seeking, it is not easily angered, it keeps no record of wrongs. Love does not delight in evil but rejoices with the truth. It always protects, always trusts, always hopes, always perseveres. Love never fails.
>
> —1 Corinthians 13:4–8, NIV

JOURNAL

7 WHAT IS A GRIEF ATTACK?

Since I've never, ever in my life experienced anything as strong as the emotions and side effects of grief, I want to describe some of what a full-blown grief attack felt like to me.

The first sensation was an irrational, overpowering feeling of complete or total loss.

My breathing would get fast and shallow; my throat would feel so "thick" that I couldn't even talk. An almost paralyzing weight would move up my entire spine, making it very difficult to even walk. My neck would feel so weak—but stiff—and my arms would be almost limp. Then, tears would shoot straight out of my eyes, causing water to run down and drip off the inside of my glasses, followed by sounds like moans and cries coming out of my mouth. I wouldn't be measuring time at this point, but as soon as I would be able to form words, I would cry out loud, "Lord, help me," over and over, and eventually the symptoms would subside.

Depending on the severity and length of the attack, I would usually recover in one to three hours. The feeling afterward was that my back, arms, shoulders, and neck would be weak and actually sore, and my head would be in a "fog." In other words, I was completely exhausted.

I'm sure that everyone's response would be different: some probably would not be nearly as severe, and some might even be more severe.

As I've said before, it was the most powerful emotional response I've ever experienced. But as terrible (and the first time, terrifying) as it was, it was still amazing what it could do to me.

JOURNAL

_____

_____

_____

_____

_____

_____

_____

_____

_____

_____

_____

_____

_____

_____

_____

_____

_____

_____

_____

_____

_____

_____

_____

_____

_____

_____

_____

_____

8 RESET, RECHARGE, REFRESH, REFOCUS

About twelve weeks after my wife's passing, I experienced my first major grief attack. It happened on what had always been a special occasion for me to celebrate—her birthday. Even in the early years of our marriage, when money was tight, I always tried to "spoil" her on that day, because I loved her. When she was no longer here, it was very hard for me to cope on her birthday. My mind just kept playing back memories of the thirty-six birthdays that I had been able to show her—in special ways—how much I cared for her.

That was the first time that the "grief waves" started crashing into me. I didn't know what was happening to me or what to do to help. I was getting emotionally and physically weaker by the minute. I needed to come up with a plan to survive—and I do mean survive—because, not knowing *what* was happening, I honestly didn't know at that point if I *would* survive. I decided to make my way through the woods, to a special place that had brought comfort to both of us in years past.

Laura had named the spot the "Cozy Corner." It's a special, beautiful place, with the calm, peaceful river to the front, a hayfield to the left, and a beautiful forest to the right. As I sat out there on a fallen log, wave after wave of grief crashed into me as I reflected on the years we had together. I was looking at the river and the steep bank leading down to it, and I thought of the story in the Bible of Elijah when he stayed alone at Brook Cherith, where God promised to care for his every need. Then, as I looked at the beautiful, lush hayfield, I thought, "He has led me beside the still waters and the green pastures," as it says in Psalm 23. Then a line or two from an old country gospel song came to mind: "Sometimes I get so weary inside, then I recall how my Jesus died."

Somehow, it helped me to realize that what I was experiencing was full-blown, powerful, and severe grief. I started thinking that when Christ died on the cross, He was bearing this grief as well as every detail of our sin, our grief, and the entire broken world that we are living in. The thought and knowledge of that didn't necessarily take away my pain and grief, but it brought comfort, as I had a deeper sense of knowing that God knew exactly what I was going through. I was definitely in need of some kind of comfort, and as I pondered what God had done for me, His Word became "comfort food" for my mind and soul.

I was probably at the "Cozy Corner" for two or three hours, as I wept, prayed, and thanked God for loving me. Eventually, a refocused spirit of thankfulness sort of "shoved" the grief to the back burner of my mind, and I slowly made my way back to the house.

I had now survived my first full-fledged, powerful grief attack, and I had gained some experience for how to survive and learn from the grief attacks that would occur in the weeks and months that followed.

As with anything we go through, experience tends to make the tough or difficult situations more tolerable, because we at least have an idea of what is happening and an idea of how long it might last. The thing that made that first grief attack so unbearable was that I really had no idea what was happening to me. After I recovered from it, I was quite amazed that grief could cause such an intense emotional response, even to the point of causing physical pain.

Second Corinthians 12:10 (NIV) says, "For when I am weak, then I am strong." That's referring to the grace that God gives us through the Holy Spirit, and in this case, His grace is strength. I'm so thankful for God's grace "to help us in our time of need" (Hebrews 4:16, NIV)!

Whether we are in an extended period of care, as Elijah was, or a one-day crisis, like I had, we can find comfort in knowing that God's grace can always help us to reset, recharge, refresh, and refocus.

JOURNAL

9 WHEN EVERYTHING IS A REMINDER

It would be a gross understatement to say that from the day Laura passed away and I started on my grief journey, many things reminded me of her. Because I think that *everything* reminded me of her. As I left the hospital alone that day—more alone than I had ever felt before—the exit door of the hospital was my first big reminder.

Several years earlier we had paid to have a handicapped-accessible, automatic door opener installed on the hospital door that we always used when entering to get her treatment each week. We did it to show gratitude to the hospital staff for always being so kind and helpful in caring for her. When Laura drove her power chair up to that door and pushed that square blue button, she found some personal satisfaction in doing something that helped others; plus, she loved the independence of letting herself in, without someone having to hold the door open for her. So as I went out that door, that square blue button was "watching" me as

I took my first solo step out the door, headed toward the first public steps of my grief journey.

As I pulled out of the parking lot, I began to see all the things and places along the way that had a memory of her attached to them. For over ten years, the trips back and forth to the hospital were about the only places we went, so we had many memorable moments and shared many conversations along that familiar route.

Then when I arrived home, the wheelchair ramp leading to the door was a reminder. Inside the house, everything in every direction was a reminder. I am thankful now more than ever that Laura and I were so close to each other. But that closeness also meant that just about every person, place, or thing that I was familiar with was also connected in some way to her. Everything that I did no longer had the time constraints that I had grown used to while caring for her. Even all the things that I no *longer* had to do in caring for her were constant reminders.

On the day of her passing and for the first several days, I don't think I realized that I was now on my grief journey. After all, the tears hadn't really started yet, probably because I was in an exhausted sort of "fog." Maybe just noticing the reminders was about all I could handle at that point.

Looking back now, I'm quite sure that the daily journaling I was doing was very helpful in taming the reminders that could have easily turned hurtful. I think that facing them every day through my writing helped me to gradually turn them into memories that I'm thankful for.

JOURNAL

10 TIME DOESN'T CARE

"He has made everything beautiful in its time" (Ecclesiastes 3:11, NIV).

When I started on my own personal grief journey, many people said, "It gets better with time." Or they would say, "Time will heal the hurt." Let me pause here and say that sayings like that provided no comfort for me at a time when I felt like my heart had been ripped out and smashed into tiny pieces.

Sayings like that made me think that if I could just pass the time, things would eventually be good again. That doesn't make any sense to me. My experience has been that I've had to take control of the time and use it to my advantage as I *work* my way through the healing process. I've not been just passively passing time, waiting for the grief to go away. I started pursuing the grief in any and every way that I could. That pursuit for me was complex and has consumed a lot of the time that I'm trying to control.

Every individual who finds himself or herself grieving will have to come up with a plan that works for him or her.

Here are some of the things I've worked on as I've continued to heal from grief.

I read every book that I could find on the grief of losing your spouse. These books didn't provide any profound advice for me, but they did help me realize that many of the "abnormal" thoughts or feelings I was having were actually very normal when someone is grieving. I also searched the Bible for verses on comfort and restoration. Then I wrote them on paper and displayed them in various places so that I could come in contact with them at different times. Something about writing out those verses was actually very hard for me to do at first, because I was hurting so badly that it was hard to believe what the promises were saying. I don't view that as lack of faith or a lack of belief in God; it's simply an example of how deep the hurt of grief is.

When I was about nine months into this journey, I joined a "Grief Share" class. This proved to be very beneficial to me, but I had to decide *when* it was the right time for me to start going, because I couldn't have enjoyed it early on.

This next one might fly in the face of what some pastors would advise, but I made a conscious decision to *not* attend church on Sunday mornings. I tried going at the beginning of my grief, but it compounded my sense of loss and really set me back even further and deeper into grief. Probably because my wife was sick for so many years, we had adapted to it, and having church at home was normal for us. Our Sunday mornings were usually awesome, and they were often the highlight of the week.

I told my pastor about my struggle, and he said, "How about Sunday night? We have a nice little service that you might enjoy." He was right. I went Sunday nights and enjoyed it! And I listened to or watched the morning service online, along with another one that my wife and I had often watched together. As a result, Sundays were once again the highlight of my week!

That's an example of how I handled something that was important to me, and the way I've worked it out has allowed me to keep moving ahead in the grieving process.

There are probably many people who would benefit from a grief support group right away or who would be comforted by being in church every time the doors were open. The point is, we each have to find a plan that works and then not give in to pressure from anyone to do something that causes more pain. My focus has been healing and less pain.

Another thing I did was to find several websites that would send daily inspirational devotions to me via e-mail. That way they were right there in front of me every morning as I checked my e-mail!

These are just a few examples of how I've been able to heal in time by controlling what I did with that time.

But don't rely on time alone to bring healing, because time doesn't care.

JOURNAL

11 THE BOX CANYON OF GRIEF

I watched an old Western movie in which a man got lost in the desert and found himself in a box canyon. When he realized that he was trapped and would have to get back out, a herd of wild horses joined him in the box canyon. Now he was *really* trapped. If he tried to scare them off, they could easily stampede him. For some reason (I know it's a movie), the horses wouldn't leave, and he was clueless about what to do.

It made me wonder if anyone had ever used an analogy like that in their personal grief journey. I used the analogy of a "skyscraper maze" (see Chapter 2: The Grief Maze) because of my dislike and actual fear of big cities. But being in a maze is still a trapped feeling, and just like the trapped man in the movie, you instantly look for and try to figure a way out.

I think that for people who have experienced deep love, grief can be very much like either of those scenarios. I also think it can sometimes be even harder for men, because we automatically try to figure out an alternate plan or try to find a way of escape. But I've learned that strong grief changes your plans, and sooner or later you discover that there is no escape.

If you are really close to your spouse and he or she is taken from you, you will have to start your own grief journey. I have been changed by mine, and you will be changed by yours.

Trust in God. He's the only one who will be with you day and night on that lonely journey.

"Trust in the Lord with all your heart.... He shall direct your paths" (Proverbs 3:5–6, NKJV).

JOURNAL

12 WHERE DID THAT COME FROM?

Speaking from my own personal experience, I can say that strong, severe grief changes you. One area of change is regarding how it affects the ways that you think and process information—or don't.

In the early days of our marriage, I started my business on a part-time basis, and after two years I incorporated and went full time with it. It was difficult, because Laura and I both had to sacrifice so much to try to help the business survive and grow. The main sacrifice we made was time with each other. We both missed each other so much, because many times I had to work over ninety hours a week. There were no cell phones then, and my shop was in another town, so it was a long-distance phone call to the house. Since we had no extra money, that meant calling home was pretty much for emergencies only.

As the years went on, the business prospered, allowing me to spend more time with Laura, and then, with her disease, it allowed me to work from home so that I could care for her full time. What a special blessing and privilege it was for us to be able to face the challenges of that disease—together. We were both thankful for the early years of sacrifice that had paid off in ways we couldn't have even imagined.

That's why it was so confusing to me that in the first few months following her passing, I was having almost nonstop thoughts that I should sell the business. I would even ask myself, "Where did *that thought* come from?"

I had read in the hospice "after care" grief guide about being careful when making major decisions during the first year of grief. So although I was aware of it, it was such a surprise to actually experience it. When I read and heard from others about those types of warnings, I thought that being logical, level-headed, and always in control of my emotions, I wouldn't be affected by thoughts or feelings like that. However, as I've discovered, the grief from losing your spouse changes many things about you.

The thoughts and feelings regarding selling the business were so strong, and they just kept coming. I was thankful that I was aware enough of where I was in the grief process that I didn't listen to the thoughts of selling. I'm sure that many people who find themselves in grief are forced to make major decisions because of the situation they find themselves in. Things such as health, finances, childcare, location, employment, and many other decisions may force some to make major changes, simply because there's no other option.

Another thing that grief did was to make me feel very abnormal. But when I experienced those major decision-impacting thoughts and feelings, they actually made me feel a little more normal, because as strange as it was, I knew that others had experienced them too! Plus, I now knew the answer to, "Where did *that thought* come from?"

It's all part of that one word—*grief.*

JOURNAL

_____

_____

_____

_____

_____

_____

_____

_____

_____

_____

_____

_____

_____

_____

_____

_____

_____

_____

_____

_____

_____

_____

_____

_____

_____

_____

_____

_____

_____

_____

_____

_____

_____

_____

_____

_____

_____

_____

_____

_____

_____

_____

_____

_____

_____

_____

_____

_____

_____

_____

13 WHAT SHOULD I SAY?

Even now, but especially at the beginning of my grief journey, the thing that I probably appreciated hearing most from others was, "I'm praying for you." There were no special or powerful phrases or even many Bible verses that gave me very much encouragement in the "early grief." In fact, some of the common things that people say at a time like that offered little comfort: "It will just take time"; "She's in a better place"; "Time will heal the hurt"; "At least you can get some rest now"; "I lost my grandmother last year, so I know what you're going through"; and "You should be happy now; she's in heaven!"

That last one—happy? Happy? Really? How could I be happy when I felt like my heart had been ripped out and smashed into tiny pieces? I remember thinking, "Yes, she's in heaven, but I'm stuck here, and that's the problem!" Plus, I was left feeling like I was only half of a person. How was I even supposed to function?

The people who offered the most comfort to me would say something like: "I can't imagine what you must be going through right now, and I want you to know that I'll pray for God to help you through this loss." And then, looking me in the eye they'd say: "And I'm serious; if you ever need to talk, call me—day or night. I probably won't have much advice, but I'll listen, and that will help me to know how to pray for you."

For me, the hardest thing to accept and adjust to was *everything*! Every place, every person, every event, every phone call, every second, minute, and hour of every day was different from before. It was like I was suddenly placed in a different culture, and I didn't even know how to communicate. Besides, since I no longer felt like a whole person, how could I even move?

All of these thoughts and emotions were so hard for me, because I had always been very logical, and I didn't have much experience with emotions. I had to wrestle with the dominant, logical part of myself that didn't want to "waste time" with emotions. But let me tell you, the emotion of grief from losing my wife of thirty-six years overpowered any and all logical thought processes I'd ever had.

Regarding the comments that are often said during a time of grief: I never really got upset or angry with any of the comments that people offered. As far as I knew, all of them were trying to offer words of encouragement during a very difficult time. I most certainly appreciated the time they took out of their schedules to try to offer comfort and support for me during the toughest time of my life.

In the past, I know there were times that I avoided people who had just suffered the loss of a very close loved one, because I didn't know what to say. I know now, after being the one standing beside the casket and shaking hands and getting hugs, that having something to say is not important. I can remember four different people who said next to nothing, but all four had tears running down their faces and dripping off their chins. The comments, comforting or not, tended to fade away. But those heartfelt tears were etched in my memory, and they were the best nonverbal comforting words that were spoken.

One thing I know now that I didn't understand before is that grief is as different as the people who go through it. You also can't measure the grief process in time or with comparisons, even if someone else's loss is similar to yours. We are all different. Therefore, the ways you find to heal will probably be different from mine.

One thing I will never again say to anyone in their grief is this: "I know what you're going through." Even if I know that person well, there is no way that I can know what he or she is going through.

Perhaps the best example we have of how to respond to someone in grief was shown to us by Jesus. When He came to the tomb of His friend Lazarus, He didn't tell the family, "He's in a better place," nor did He offer any other nice saying. Lazarus was His friend too, and when He got there, "Jesus wept" (John 11:35, NKJV). Jesus experienced grief—as a man—and He wept! That verse, known for being the shortest verse in the Bible, is so special to me now, because I know that Jesus experienced grief. Because Jesus knows me better than I know myself, I can ask for comfort, in His name, and the Holy Spirit will comfort me, because, He *does* know what I'm going through.

Now there's encouragement!

JOURNAL

My Grief Journey: Stories and Illustrations

_____
_____
_____
_____
_____
_____
_____
_____
_____
_____
_____
_____
_____
_____
_____
_____
_____
_____
_____
_____
_____
_____
_____
_____
_____
_____

14 THE PRINT SHOP BLEW UP!

When I was in high school, I was fortunate enough to learn about (and get some hands-on experience with) an old printing press that was in a print-shop room in the basement of the school. There were drawers and drawers of type—individual letters in various shapes, sizes, and fonts. There were also drawers with images, spacers, and the frames where you would manually "set" each individual letter, punctuation mark, image, spacer, etc. Then the completed frame would be mounted into the press, and with constant attention—involving ink and the placement and removal of papers—you could print posters or whatever was needed.

I never would have thought that almost forty years after the printing press experience, the grief from losing my wife would cause me to reflect on that print shop. But one of the picture-story scenarios that was in my mind when I was trying to figure out how to function after my wife passed away came from my memories of that shop.

It was as if the entire print shop of my thought processes had "blown up!" It seemed like all the different sizes of letters that made up all the words and memories, all the spacers between events, and the frames that held all the type from our thirty-six years together were in a huge pile, and nobody but me was allowed to sort and reorganize the "mess." Plus, since it represented my life and time with Laura, I knew that I was the only one who could reorganize it. "But how? Where will I even start? I don't remember how the drawers were set up, and I am afraid that if I start, I'll do it all wrong."

Knowing that it was *my* grief journey and *my* print shop, I started putting individual letters in compartments and drawers, knowing that it's not possible for anyone to put it all back together the way it used to be. The first few weeks and months of working with the "mess" consisted of trying different methods of sorting and organizing the pieces that represented my thoughts and memories of the years I had with my wife. There were times I felt overwhelmed and didn't think I'd be able to do the job. I was continually asking God to give me the strength, the ability, and the wisdom to help me make some kind of order of the messed-up "type" that represented my memories as well as the hopes and dreams that could no longer be.

As the months of tedious work continued, I started to notice that the "mess" was truly getting organized, and even though everything in the print shop of my mind was now in a different location, I was slowly learning the new systems. One thing that continued to make it difficult was that there were a lot of pieces missing; they were not here; they were gone—lost. Even the drawers that once contained those pieces were gone. Those drawers contained the type to print "memories of Steve and Laura." What a reminder that we will never again "print" any memories together.

Everything is certainly getting more organized, but I'm still having trouble getting used to all the changes in the way things are set up now.

As time goes on, I'm thinking that even though that press is old and outdated, who knows, it might be fun to try to work with it again someday!

"Behold, all things have become new" (2 Corinthians 5:17, NKJV).

JOURNAL

15 GRIEF AT ONE YEAR

One year ago this very moment, the barrier between me and my emotions was removed. That was the moment Laura left my arms and was taken by her angel escort to the arms of Jesus. What an incredible moment that was for her! But what a painful moment it was for me and for the others who loved her.

I am not grieving "as those who have no hope" or as those who have no love and therefore don't grieve at all. But I am absolutely amazed at how powerful this emotion of grief is and how complex its details are. I've watched as the "grief maze" that I entered that day went from a dark, intimidating, and lonely place with skyscraper walls to a much brighter and no-longer-intimidating place. God is leading me through it, and He's never left me—although I've left Him at times by lagging behind or by sometimes going forward without Him. But I'm trying to move at His speed, even if it means that sometimes He has to carry me because I'm too weak to move. I'm constantly reminded that I'm *not* able, but He *is* able.

This place I'm in has been a lonely place, because I have had limited contact with others compared to what it was like with Laura here. But the solitude has been a necessary part of this grief journey that I'm on. God said: "Be still, and know that I am God" (Psalm 46:10, NKJV). Sometimes extended periods of loneliness, stillness, and quietness are necessary to remind me that He is in control. Plus, it was necessary for me to be able to process the grief and get back some order for my fragmented self-worth. I also believe that in this quietness, "The Lord has heard the voice of my weeping" (Psalm 6:8, NKJV).

When will this extended period of quiet and solitude end? I don't know. I'm confident it will at some point as new activities, friends, and relationships occur. God knows me *far* better than I know myself (and that has really been made known to me this past year). So I'll try to do my best to move forward at His speed—not mine.

JOURNAL

16 RECIPE FOR REGRET

As I observe people now—differently from how I would have before this journey—I constantly see people in a big rush to go nowhere and accomplish nothing. So many are busy acquiring things and doing things that will add nothing to their lives or even have a chance of becoming a memory that will become a legacy. Sadly, they are following a recipe for regret.

During the nearly twelve years that I cared for my wife in her declining health, I made a decision to focus on her and personally care for her as much as I possibly could. I could have easily hired health-care workers to assist with her care—and several people told me at the time that hiring help with her care would be a wise thing to do. But by pouring myself into personally caring for Laura's every need and learning nearly every medical detail about her condition, I was able to get close to her innermost feelings and enjoy a closeness that most never experience. Because I chose to give up whatever plans I had for myself and focus on her care, God gave me a wonderful sense of contentment, because I knew that I was doing what God wanted me to do!

Aside from the satisfying sense of accomplishment that I received from caring for her, the benefit I'm experiencing now is this: *I have no regrets.* What an unexpected blessing that has been to me in my grief. As I've heard others talk about their grief journeys, regrets seem to be a major obstacle for some of them.

This grief is the toughest thing I've ever experienced, and I still have a long road of emotional healing to travel. But regrets involve the past and other people or things that you can't change. Besides, think about it: I could have stayed as busy as possible, and it would have provided nothing that matters and no memories. But I have awesome memories with love attached, and those memories may represent the greatest accomplishment of my life! I am so thankful for the contentment God provided for me and the strength He gave me while caring for Laura during the years of her disease.

"For I have learned to be content whatever the circumstances" (Philippians 4:11, NIV).

JOURNAL

17 NOT SO SPECIAL, SPECIAL DAYS

"Love lasts, and what love does will last."
—W. W. Wiersbe

Valentine's Day—the first one without Laura in thirty-eight years. Overall, it wasn't that bad of a day. Both Laura and I were very practical, something we probably learned because for the first ten years of our marriage, money was so tight that we *had* to be practical! She thought flowers were a waste of money—except for one time: when she was finally confined to bed and a wheelchair, she was worried that I wouldn't think she was pretty anymore. So for Valentine's Day I called the florist and ordered eleven roses. Using words from a Hank Williams Jr. song of the same name, the card read: "I guess you noticed there's only eleven roses. I chose them from this florist just for you. If you take them and look into the mirror, the twelfth rose will be looking back at you." She absolutely loved it, and she never again worried that she wasn't pretty to me. (And just so you know, I *always* thought she was beautiful!)

There were a few times that I was able to get her some jewelry. The most special time was when I had a ring made for her that had a big diamond in the center, a ruby on each side of the diamond, and several smaller diamonds spreading down the sides of the two rubies. When I gave it to her I told her what it represented: "The big diamond represents Christ; the two rubies represent both of us; and the smaller diamonds represent our friends. And we are all centered around Christ." That meant so much to her. She would often show people the ring, and several times she used the opportunity to tell others of her relationship with Christ. I was surprised at times to see her just staring at it and to hear her comment on how beautiful it was.

Most times though, we didn't really get or do anything special on occasions like the lesser holidays. She would usually say, "I have Christ, and I have you. What more do I really need?"

So even though some of the "special" days like Valentine's Day might not have seemed too special, they were wonderful to us and have provided great memories for me on this grief journey I'm traveling.

JOURNAL

_____

_____

_____

_____

_____

_____

_____

_____

_____

_____

_____

_____

_____

_____

_____

_____

_____

_____

_____

_____

_____

_____

_____

_____

_____

_____

_____

18 FANTASYLAND

During the first several months of my grief journey, there were times I almost felt as if I were in some sort of a strange reversal of a fantasy movie. Remember *It's a Wonderful Life* with Jimmy Stewart as George Bailey? There are also some newer ones with a similar theme: where the person is the same, but everything and everyone around him or her is different, and nobody knows that individual. That's the way I felt sometimes— only in reverse. It seemed that all my surroundings and those around me were all the same, but I was different and didn't know how to react or respond.

The world in which I looked the same no longer looked the same to me. I remember thinking, "Why is everything and everyone going so fast?" My world had screeched to a halt and was turned upside down. Feeling like I was only half a person, I wondered how I was going to figure all of this out. Even at home, I sometimes wondered, "Who am I?" because things like the TV shows that Laura and I used to watch together no longer had any appeal to me. On top of all the painful grief, all of these thoughts and feelings were so confusing. At that point, I hadn't yet realized that I was on my own personal grief journey. By personal, I mean that it was for me only, and there was no way to process the grief other than to proceed on that journey.

Everyone responds to grief differently, and I've said that many times before. But it is a simple fact that I probably should have known before—but I didn't.

When it seemed like everything else was moving so fast, I felt like I was wearing lead boots, and there was no way I was going to be able to catch up or keep up with everything. What I hadn't realized yet was that the feeling of being in some type of backward fantasy movie was really a glimpse of my new reality. I was still looking at and responding to everything as though Laura were still part of my life. The reality was that even though she was in my memories, she was no longer here in person. That meant that I *would* be different. I *had to be* different; otherwise, there would be no way to discover the healing that I've been finding on this grief journey.

Yes, a new reality is where my grief journey is leading me, because my former reality with Laura is completed. So if I don't keep moving toward my new reality, then the only other place I could be would be to remain in grief. Grief is the most painful, life-controlling emotion I've ever experienced, so I certainly do not want to have a permanent identity with grief.

I now realize that this grief journey has been mainly for healing and for understanding some of the many changes I'm facing. I'm also slowly accepting the fact that I'm not a "half," and that the number *one* is a whole number. It takes a lot of effort and energy to travel this grief journey. That's why I'm thankful that I always have help.

"He gives strength to the weary and increases the power of the weak" (Isaiah 40:29, NIV).

JOURNAL

19 THE SCAVENGER HUNT

When I was a child, my parents had an Easter tradition of a scavenger hunt. They would prepare an individual "hunt," with clues, for each of my siblings and me. The hunts were customized with consideration for the age, capabilities, and knowledge of each child. As we came downstairs on Easter Sunday morning, there would be a small note for each of us. It had our name at the top and contained a message. Each one of us would then start our individual scavenger hunt. That was our total focus until we gathered all the clues that led us to the prize at the completion.

I remember clues like: "Go look on top of the water heater." The next said, "Go look on the top shelf of your closet." Then: "Go look on the vise on the workbench in the garage." "Go look in your sock drawer." Finally, "Go look in the trunk of the car." And there was a bag of candy with my name on it!

After Laura and I were married, I told her about those Easter scavenger hunts, and she said that she had never done that before. So on our first Easter, I sent her on her first scavenger hunt! She tried to act embarrassed, but the smile on her face and the excitement she displayed told me that she enjoyed it. It was only necessary and special to do that for her one time, but it made a great memory that we talked about for years—and it has provided a treasured memory for me now that she's gone.

As I make my way on this grief journey, there have certainly been days when I have felt as though I were on some type of scavenger hunt. But instead of a fun adventure, this hunt has sometimes felt like some sort of twisted brain teaser: like the days when I'm looking for clues that don't exist, hoping they will lead me to a prize that I know doesn't exist.

Yet, as I've worked on processing my grief, there have been days that could have been described pretty easily by the scavenger-hunt analogy. For me, the hunt would represent the patterns and habits that *we* formed for solving problems or for approaching situations and that were developed over the first thirty-six years of my adult life. Now it's no longer *we* or *us* on the hunt. It's just *me* or *I*, so everything that my brain was programmed to do as a normal response is now completely different.

The saying, "Old habits die hard," certainly applies to me on this grief journey, as just about everything in my life has had to find a new normal. As I continue to heal, I'm spending less time on those "old-habits" scavenger hunts, but sometimes I catch myself thinking in the *we* or *us* mode, and it can still send me on one.

I definitely need new understanding for so many things. That's why I need to follow what Proverbs 3:5 (NIV) teaches: "Trust in The Lord with all your heart, and lean not on your own understanding."

JOURNAL

20 THE ATTACK DOG OR LAP DOG OF GRIEF

There were times on my grief journey when I was ambushed by what I thought of as "the attack dog of grief." I would be having a fairly normal, maybe even mundane, type of day, when suddenly I was emotionally cornered by an "attack dog." That's when those emotions—more powerful than anything I have ever experienced—would grip me like the jaws of an attack dog. I compared it to an attack dog, because it was a very frightening, life-controlling event. I obviously did not like grief having such power over my emotions. So that was when I decided to go after grief, and I got serious about my journey.

I've had some people tell me that my grief journey will last the rest of my life. If that's in reference to recurring thoughts and memories of my wife and the time we had together, then yes, I agree with that, because that will always be a part of who I am. But I plan on those thoughts and memories being pleasant and happy, not filled with the sadness and sorrow that I associate with grief. So with what I've learned thus far, I don't agree that this grief journey that I've been on will in fact last the rest of my life. This is something that I've poured the majority of my thoughts into, with a goal of completing this painful, sad, and sorrowful journey. If there were no chance or hope of having some sort of completion to this, then why bother? Because as I've explored the depths and details of a deep, complex, loving relationship like we had, it leaves me absolutely exhausted at times. Why? Because it is very hard work!

At the start of this journey, I focused on wanting it to go away, because it hurt so badly. But I'm finding out that I have to pursue the grief so that I can understand it, and then I will be able to control or maybe even conquer the grief. By doing that, I believe that I will be able to enjoy anything without the fear of stirring up sorrow in relation to certain memories or feelings.

So as I continue to pursue and learn the tactics of hurtful grief, I will gain control of it and transform that attack dog into a harmless lap dog.

"Perfect love casts out fear" (1 John 4:18, NKJV).

JOURNAL

21 ARE WE THERE YET?

It's been over one year now that I've been on this grief journey. For me, the hardest part of this has been the profound silence from no longer being able to communicate with my wife. I caught myself, many times, on the way to share something with Laura, when it hit me—again—that she was no longer here. It was those times especially that caused me to lose control of my emotions and caused me to realize that this would be a long journey. It was the days like those that made me feel like I didn't understand much about this journey at all.

When that strong feeling of loss came back, it felt like a brand new and complete loss. That just didn't line up with reality, and I would be aware of that, but that total loss would still hit, and believe me, it hit hard. Throughout our marriage, whatever problem we faced, I would always figure it out and fix it. That was part of what made this so difficult, because I was trying to figure out and fix something that had no normal solution. It was so hard to not just go about my normal routine of coming up with a solution. My brain felt like it was in sections, and all the sections weren't necessarily in agreement with the way this grief journey was going.

Picture the sections of my brain all going on this journey together. The majority of my brain represents the adults that are driving, watching all the road signs and directions. Then there are some smaller sections that keep yelling, "Are we there yet?" That always catches the majority sections off guard, because the only response they can come up with is, "We don't know, because we don't really know where we're going."

If you've been there, you understand. If you have not, you're probably thinking, "How messed up is that?"

Well, I'm still on my grief journey, and things are looking brighter, so I'm getting closer. But no, I'm not there yet.

JOURNAL

22 GOD DOES NOT WASTE PAIN

My wife, Laura, endured long-term, chronic, severe pain. That pain, combined with profound weakness, eventually stopped her from even moving, because she was confined to bed twenty-four hours a day. But even in the depths of that severe pain, she would always say, "God does not waste pain." She would also say, "Whatever your circumstances are, use them to glorify God, because it's amazing what God can do."

I witnessed many incredible events and opportunities during our years together that indeed proved both of her statements to be true. But when I experienced the life-controlling, event-changing, severe pain of grief, I thought, "Here's some pain that God is going to waste."

It was so intense all the time, especially during those first few months. I felt embarrassed and ashamed that I was crying so much, because to me it demonstrated a weakness in myself that I had never known. Then, as I considered that second statement Laura made, I thought, "There's no way to glorify God with this grief."

But then I recalled the early days of Laura's illness: there were times she struggled terribly with accepting her limitations and pain. She had to learn the lessons God was teaching her before He could use her pain for His glory. My circumstances were certainly different, but I realized that I had a lot to learn about grief and my new self before God could use my pain and receive glory from it.

Throughout my life, I never wanted to be a victim, and I never wanted anything to control me. My grief journey was so different from anything I had ever imagined or experienced, and I did not want to be a long-term victim of grief and have my life controlled by it. Grief is amazing—in a bad way. Healing from grief is amazing—in a good way! I'm sure I still have much more to learn on my grief journey, so that means I'm still *on* that journey.

I want to finish these stories and illustrations with a quotation that describes where I'm at on this journey:

> Now this is not the end. It is not even the beginning of the end. But it is, perhaps, the end of the beginning.

> —Winston Churchill

JOURNAL

ABOUT THE AUTHOR

Steve Nauman was born in rural Chenango County, New York. He has one brother and five sisters. Steve's father, Arnold, owned and operated a general store, while his mother, Patricia, worked at home, caring for the children and all the related household chores.

Steve started working part time in his father's store at the age of seven and worked there full time for two years after high school. In 1977, at the age of twenty, he moved to Elkhart, Indiana, where he started dating Laura. They married in 1978.

In the early 1980s, Steve started Mid America Screw (MAS) Products, Inc., which he still owns today and where he currently serves as president. He lives on a farm in nearby Goshen, where he enjoys his horses and experiments with various methods of organic gardening. Some of his other interests include old-time country and bluegrass gospel music, classic cars, and nature, which he often refers to as "bird, brook, and blossom."

To contact the author, Steve Nauman:

NaumanBook@gmail.com

Made in the USA
Middletown, DE
12 July 2015